W9-CLC-917

TANA HOBAN
Animal, Vegetable, or Mineral?

GREENWILLOW BOOKS NEW YORK

The full-color photographs were reproduced from 35-mm slides. The text type is Kabel.

Printed in Hong Kong by South China Printing Company (1988) Ltd.
First Edition   10 9 8 7 6 5 4 3 2 1

Library of Congress Cataloging-in-Publication Data

Hoban, Tana.
Animal, vegetable, or mineral? / by Tana Hoban.
    p.   cm.
ISBN 0-688-12746-0 (trade).   0-688-12747-9 (lib. bdg.)
1. Science—Pictorial works—Juvenile literature.   2. Natural history—Pictorial works—Juvenile literature.   [1. Natural history—Pictorial works.]   I. Title.   Q163.H57   1995
508'.022'2—dc20   94-20904   CIP   AC

ANIMAL, VEGETABLE, OR MINERAL?

ANIMAL KINGDOM: The one of the three basic groups of natural objects that comprises all living and extinct animals.

PLANT KINGDOM: The one of the three basic groups of natural objects that comprises all living and extinct plants.

MINERAL KINGDOM: The one of the three basic groups of natural objects that comprises inorganic objects.

—Merriam Webster's Collegiate Dictionary, Tenth Edition

Remembering Eddie